Congratulations, _____!

This page holds my warmest words of encouragement, heartfelt wishes, and continued support as you start this wonderful journey.

*To New Beginnings*

To the champions of learning,
setting sail with boundless dedication,
igniting the flame of passion and
unlocking endless potential
in the world of education.
Welcome aboard!

*HDM*

To New Beginnings:
Embracing the A, B, and C's of Your
First Year Teaching

Text Copyright © 2024 Holly DiBella-McCarthy

All rights reserved. Published by Book Chatter Press.
P.O. Box 1474, Little River, SC 29566
bookchatterpress.com
hollydibellamccarthy.com

ISBN:979-8-9883308-9-9

# Contents

*"... a new teacher's companion, confidante, and source of inspiration."*

APPLAUD    9

BEGIN    15

CREATE CONNECTIONS    23

COMMUNICATE CONFIDENTLY    35

COURAGE    41

QUOTES    45

BENEFITS    49

KID QUOTES    53

MY CLASS KID QUOTES    57

NOTEWORTHY    95

Welcome to the most rewarding and challenging profession on Earth!

As you embark on your journey into the wonderful world of teaching, prepare yourself for an adventure filled with laughter, learning, and unexpected surprises.

*To New Beginnings*

Get ready for a wild ride filled with
ups and downs,
twists and turns,
and moments of sheer joy and frustration.

Your first year of teaching will be a
whirlwind of emotions, challenges,
and growth opportunities.

Embrace the chaos, stay resilient,
and never lose sight of why
you chose this noble profession.

Remember, teaching is not just a job;
it's a calling, a privilege,
and a tremendous responsibility.
You have the power to shape the future,
one student at a time.

So, buckle up, hold on tight, and get ready to
make a difference!

# Let's Dive into the A, B & C's of Surviving Your First Year

All right, newcomer, it's time to roll up your sleeves and dive into the ABCs of thriving in your debut year in the classroom.

From assessing your teaching skills to building connections with colleagues and students, setting up your classroom for success, to navigating parent communication with confidence, we've got you covered.

So, take a deep breath,
embrace the challenge,
and let's dive in!

*"Every expert was once a beginner."*
**- Helen Hayes**

# APPLAUD

# Celebrate Your Brilliance:

## Picasso of Pedagogy and Emerging Maestro

As you step into your role as a new teacher, it's natural to feel a mix of excitement and trepidation.

You've spent years honing your skills in curriculum, assessment, lesson planning, methodology, and supporting students with special education needs.

Yet, the journey of learning never truly ends. Take a moment to applaud where you stand on this continuum of growth.

*"Teaching is the greatest act of optimism."*
**- Colleen Wilcox**

Reflect on your experiences,
both inside and outside the classroom,
and consider how they have shaped you
as an educator.

Write down the areas where you feel confident
in your abilities, celebrating your strengths and
acknowledging the hard work that has
brought you to this point.

Use the following pages to jot down these
affirmations, reinforcing your belief in your
capabilities and setting a positive tone
for the journey ahead.

*"You have within you right now, everything you
need to deal with whatever the world
can throw at you."*
**- Brian Tracy**

KUDOS TO ME BECAUSE I . . .

*To New Beginnings*

# KUDOS TO ME BECAUSE I . . .

While it's tempting to emulate the teachers who have inspired you, remember that you bring your own unique perspective and strengths to the table.

Embrace the opportunity to carve out your own path, drawing upon the lessons you've learned and the insights you've gained along the way. Identify the areas where you feel less confident or in need of further development.

Commit to seeking out opportunities for growth, whether through professional development workshops, mentorship programs, or collaborative partnerships with colleagues.

By actively seeking ways to strengthen your skills, you demonstrate a growth mindset and lay the groundwork for a fulfilling and successful career in education.

*"Teaching is a profession where you're always learning, and that's the most exciting part."*
**- Erin Gruwell**

# BEGIN

# Cue the Confetti:
## Celebrating Your Achievement
(You Deserve It!)

Congratulations, new teacher, on reaching this milestone in your journey!

Take a moment to celebrate your achievement and bask in the excitement of becoming a teacher.

You've worked hard, overcome challenges, and pursued your passion for education with unwavering determination.

So, cue the confetti, pop the champagne, and celebrate this momentous occasion with friends, family, and fellow educators. You deserve it!

*"Education is the key to success in life, and teachers make a lasting impact in the lives of their students."*
**- Solomon Ortiz**

# Panic Mode:
## Preparing for Your First Year
(Don't Worry, We've Got You Covered)

Feeling overwhelmed by the thought of your first year of teaching?

Don't panic! With careful planning, preparation, and a dash of humor, you'll conquer any challenge that comes your way.

Start by familiarizing yourself with the curriculum, school policies, and resources available to you.

Create a daily schedule, organize your classroom materials, and stock up on essential supplies.

Remember, you're not alone on this journey. Reach out to mentors, colleagues, and online communities for support and guidance.

*"You gain strength, courage, and confidence by every experience in which you really stop to look fear in the face."*
**- Eleanor Roosevelt**

# Setting Up Your Classroom for Success

(Warning: May Involve a Lot of Pinterest)

Get ready to unleash your creativity and transform your classroom into a vibrant and welcoming learning environment.

From colorful bulletin boards to cozy reading nooks, the possibilities are endless!

Consider your teaching style, students' interests, and educational goals as you design your classroom layout and décor.

Don't be afraid to think outside the box, experiment with different arrangements, and incorporate student input into the design process. And don't forget, a little bit of Pinterest inspiration never hurt anyone!

*"Organizing is what you do before you do something so that when you do it, it's not all mixed up."*
**- A.A. Milne**

# My Classroom Layout

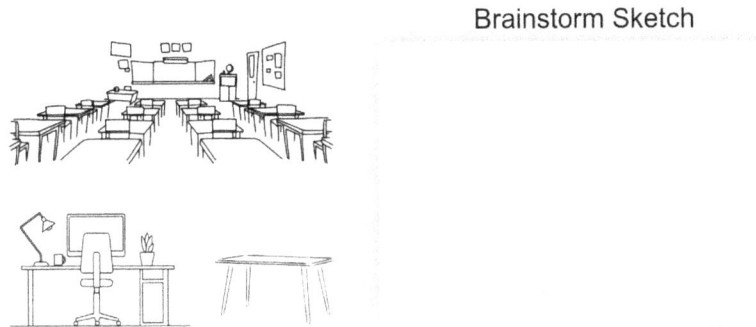

Brainstorm Sketch

Brainstorm Sketch

Final Layout Plan (I think!)

# Recall the SPED-tacular:

A Humorous Guide to Mastering Special Education Lingo for Gen Ed Teachers Before the School Year Begins

**Sped-tacular**: When something in the classroom goes beyond ordinary and becomes truly special education magic, it's officially Sped-tacular! Get ready to witness those unforgettable moments that make teaching an adventure.

**IEP-IDEA**: No, it's not a funky dance move; it's an Individualized Education Program (IEP). Embrace the creativity and personalized touch that comes with tailoring education plans to meet every student's unique needs.

**Inclusion Fiesta**: Imagine a classroom where everyone's invited to the party! Inclusion Fiesta celebrates diversity and togetherness, ensuring every student feels like a valued class member.

**Sensory Safari**: Welcome to the wild world of sensory exploration! From squishy stress balls to cozy sensory corners, embark on a sensory safari where learning engages all the senses.

**ABCs of ASD**: It's not just the alphabet; it's the ABCs of Autism Spectrum Disorder (ASD). Learn to navigate the spectrum with patience, understanding, and a whole lot of heart.

**PARA-mazing**: Shoutout to the unsung heroes of the classroom – the paras! They're the real MVPs who provide invaluable support and make the teaching journey truly PARA-mazing.

**SPED Talk**: Get ready for some serious SPED Talk – the language of special education where acronyms abound and collaboration reigns supreme. Dive in, decode the jargon, and join the conversation!

**Resource Rockstar**: Who needs a superhero cape when you can be a Resource Rockstar? Whether adapting materials or finding innovative solutions, embrace your inner Rockstar and make learning accessible to all.

**Accommodation Fiesta**: It's time to party with accommodations! From preferential seating to extended time, Accommodation Fiesta ensures that every student has what they need to shine.

**Inclusive Huddle**: Gather 'round for the Inclusive Huddle. Join forces with colleagues, students, and families to create a supportive and inclusive learning community.

So, grab your cape and your sense of humor because every day is an adventure in the world of special education!

# Student Modifications & Accommodations PLANNER

## STUDENTS INITIALS AND NEEDED CLASSROOM ACCOMMODATIONS

## COLLABORATION PARTNERS

### NAMES OF SUPPORT STAFF

- 
- 
- 
- 
- 
- 

### COLLABORATION SCHEDULE

### STUDENTS WITH IEP'S

### STUDENTS WITH 504 PLANS

# CREATE CONNECTIONS

# Networking 101:
## Building Relationships within the School Community

(It's Like College All Over Again)

Just like in college, building relationships within your new school community is essential for success.

Take the time to introduce yourself to the secretary, custodian, school nurse, cafeteria staff, and other administrators, teachers and support staff.

These connections will not only provide support and guidance but also help foster a sense of belonging and collaboration.

Bear in mind that the school is not just a workplace; it's a community where everyone plays a vital role in the educational journey.

*"Coming together is a beginning, staying together is progress, and working together is success."*
**– Henry Ford**

Additionally, embracing the opportunity to really get to know all adults who contribute to the school's success can have numerous benefits.

When you take an interest in others' hobbies, pets, or family members they often talk about, it helps build rapport and creates a more positive work environment.

By showing genuine curiosity and asking about their interests outside of work, you can strengthen connections and foster a sense of camaraderie.

Use the next pages to write down names and conversation starters, ensuring you're prepared to engage in meaningful interactions and cultivate lasting relationships within the school community.

*"Alone we can do so little; together we can do so much."*
**- Helen Keller**

# MY SCHOOL COMMUNITY

## MY SCHOOL COMMUNITY

## Colleagues:
### Your New Squad
(or Partners in Hilarious Staff Room Banter)

Your colleagues can be your greatest allies in the teaching profession. Choose wisely! Surround yourself with positive, supportive, and collaborative individuals who share your passion for education and are committed to student success.

Seek out mentorship opportunities, collaborate on lesson planning and curriculum development, and share resources and ideas with your fellow teachers.

Remember, teamwork makes the dream work! Is there an opportunity to observe other teachers working with students, perhaps during your planning time? Do it! And consider slipping a thank you note to them including the positive things you observed.

*"Surround yourself with only people who are going to lift you higher."*
**- Oprah Winfrey**

# Humor, Empathy, and No Bribery:
## The Recipe for Classroom Success

Building positive relationships with your students is the key to a successful classroom environment.

The first week or two of school should prioritize getting to know your students and establishing strong classroom management.

Keep in mind that you are not a camp counselor; you are a teacher your students must respect. If they respect you and the classroom rules and expectations, they will like you better than their camp counselor.

*"Students don't care how much you know until they know how much you care."*
- John C. Maxwell

Consistency,
in rules and expectations is crucial. Get to know your students as individuals, learn their names, interests, and strengths, and show genuine care and concern for their well-being.

Use humor, empathy, and positive reinforcement to create a supportive and nurturing learning environment where students feel valued, respected, and motivated to succeed.

And always remember, a little bit of humor goes a long way, but bribery is not the answer!

*"As educators, our role is to create an environment where students can thrive academically and emotionally. Consistency in our approach fosters trust and confidence in our students, paving the way for meaningful learning experiences."*
**- Marva Collins**

# The Great Classroom Tug-of-War:

## Why Teachers Should Not Pick up the Rope!

First off, engaging in power struggles with students is like trying to teach a cat to fetch – it's a futile effort, and you're likely to end up scratching your head in bewilderment.

But fear not—Here is your reminder about why it's time to drop that metaphorical rope and save your sanity!

Picture this: you're facing your first class, feeling like a deer in headlights. Suddenly, a student decides to test your authority, and you're on the brink of a showdown.

But here's the deal: you don't have to play that game. Instead of getting sucked into a power struggle, set clear rules from the get-go.

*"Effective classroom management is based on the teacher's ability to establish authority through positive student-teacher relationships."*

**- Fred Jones**

Offer choices within those boundaries, like letting kids choose between two activities.

Let's say young Johnny is digging in his heels about an assignment. Instead of butting heads, give him options like tackling the task in a different way or trying an alternative activity. That way, he feels like he's in the driver's seat, not just a passenger on the struggle bus.

Positive reinforcement is your secret weapon – praise the good stuff and watch the magic happen. When your students are rocking it – whether it's participating like champs, cooperating like pros, or giving it their all – shower them with compliments and rewards. It's like sprinkling fairy dust on their confidence and motivation.

*"Successful behavior management starts with building strong relationships with students. When students feel connected and respected, they are more likely to cooperate."*
**- Dr. Marvin Marshall**

Every behavior has a reason. Before you react, take a moment to figure out what's driving it.

Behind every eye roll and defiant stance lies a story waiting to be uncovered. So, instead of engaging in a battle royale, channel your inner superhero and address the root cause of the behavior. Maybe Xavier is acting out because he's dying for a bit of attention or itching to show off his independence. Is Taylor acting out because she's secretly a math genius trapped in a world of long division? Maybe it's time to unleash her inner mathlete with some brain-busting challenges.

Tuning into the why behind their antics can defuse the situation faster than a balloon at a porcupine party.

*"Consistency is the key to effective classroom management. Students thrive on predictability and routine."*
**- Lee Canter**

So, there you have it—my best advice
for managing those little Power
Struggle Wannabees.

Do not pick up that rope,
dish out the choices,
spread the love, and play detective
with those behaviors.

You've got this!

"Handle power struggles by offering
choices, love, and detective
work—never pick up the rope."
**Holly DiBella-McCarthy**

# COMMUNICATE CONFIDENTLY

# Parent Communication:
## You Can Do This!

(Even If It Means Perfecting Your
Parent Whisperer Technique)

Effective communication with parents is essential for student success. Keep parents informed about classroom activities, assignments, and student progress through newsletters, emails, or phone calls.

Be proactive in addressing parents' concerns or questions and strive to maintain open and transparent communication channels.

Regardless of whether you agree with their parenting philosophy, you need to respect it. No matter what it is, remember they love their child more than you do. Step into their shoes and find a way to connect with every parent; after all, collaboration between home and school is key to student achievement!

*"In the dance between teacher and parent, consistency of communication builds the rhythm of success."*
**- Holly DiBella-McCarthy**

# Open House Survival Guide:
## Navigating Awkward Conversations Like a Pro

Open house can be a nerve-wracking experience for new teachers, but fear not! With a little bit of preparation and a whole lot of confidence, you'll navigate those awkward conversations like a pro.

Prepare a welcoming and informative presentation about your classroom expectations, curriculum, and teaching philosophy.

Be approachable, enthusiastic, and eager to answer parents' questions. And don't forget to smile, relax, and enjoy the opportunity to showcase your passion for teaching!

*"The art of communication is the language of leadership."*
**- James Humes**

# How to Talk So Kids Will Listen... and Maybe Even Learn Something

Communication is the cornerstone of effective teaching. Develop clear, concise, and engaging communication strategies to captivate your students' attention and convey important information effectively.

Use active listening techniques, ask open-ended questions, and encourage student participation and discussion in the classroom.

Create a supportive and inclusive learning environment where students feel comfortable expressing themselves and sharing their ideas. Individualizing for each student is imperative; tailor your communication to meet every learner's unique needs and preferences, fostering a deeper connection and understanding.

*"The single biggest problem in communication is the illusion that it has taken place."*
— George Bernard Shaw

# Connecting with Every Student:
## Embracing Diversity in the Classroom

In teaching, it's essential to recognize and celebrate the diversity of students' needs and abilities, including those with special education needs.

Whether they are integrated full-time or just for a short period of time in your class, these students require connection and a sense of belonging within the classroom community.

It's imperative to establish a regular system of communication with their special education case manager to stay informed about their individualized education plans (IEPs) and any specific accommodations or modifications they may require.

*"Teaching is the one profession that creates all other professions."*
**– Unknown**

Remember,
reaching out to students with different learning needs requires communication with additional support staff, such as speech pathologists, occupational therapists, physical therapists, vision and hearing specialists, school nurses or school psychologists who will provide valuable insights into how you can create a supportive and inclusive learning environment tailored to their needs.

By fostering genuine connections and understanding, you can ensure that every student feels valued, respected, and empowered to thrive in
your classroom.

*"Every child deserves a champion – an adult who will never give up on them, who understands the power of connection and insists that they become the best that they can possibly be."*
**- Rita Pierson**

# COURAGE

# Embracing Challenges as Opportunities

(Or How to Pretend You Know What You're Doing)

As a new teacher, you'll face countless challenges and obstacles along the way. Welcome them with courage, resilience, and a healthy dose of humor.

View challenges as opportunities for growth, learning, and innovation. Don't be afraid to take risks, try new strategies, and step out of your comfort zone. And remember, it's okay to ask for help when you need it. You're not expected to have all the answers, but you are expected to face challenges head-on with confidence and determination.

Communication is a two-way street. Be open to feedback, flexible in your approach, and always willing to adapt and improve.

*"Success is not final, failure is not fatal: It is the courage to continue that counts."*
**- Winston Churchill**

## Fake It 'Til You Make It:

### Continuous Learning and Professional Development

(Google Is Your Best Friend)

Nobody expects you to have all the answers as a new teacher. Embrace the philosophy of "fake it 'til you make it" and approach each day as an opportunity to learn and grow.

Take advantage of professional development opportunities, attend workshops and conferences, and seek out mentorship and guidance from experienced educators.

And when in doubt, remember that Google is your best friend. There's a wealth of resources, lesson plans, and teaching tips just a click away!

*"The only source of knowledge is experience."*
**- Albert Einstein**

## Standing Up for Your Students:

(Because Somebody's Gotta Do It)

As a teacher, you are not just an educator; you are an advocate for your students. Stand up for their rights, their needs, and their voices. Challenge injustice, promote equity and inclusion, and create a safe and supportive learning environment where all students feel valued, respected, and empowered to succeed.

Be their voice in the classroom, the school, and the community. Sometimes the greatest act of courage is simply showing up and being there for your students when they need you most.

*"Our lives begin to end the day we become silent about things that matter."*
**- Martin Luther King Jr.**

# QUOTES

from Experienced Teachers . . .

# Inspirational Quotes to Motivate and Encourage

(Because Sometimes You Need a Pep Talk)

*"In teaching, you cannot see the fruit of a day's work. It is invisible and remains so, maybe for twenty years."*

**- Jacques Barzun**

Teaching is a labor of love that often goes unnoticed and unappreciated. But remember, every lesson taught, every smile shared, and every "aha" moment experienced leaves a lasting impact on your students' lives. Keep pushing forward, stay resilient, and never lose sight of the difference you're making, one day at a time.

# Words of Wisdom to Reflect On

(Or Just Laugh About)

*"The art of teaching is the art of assisting discovery."*

**- Mark Van Doren**

Teaching is not about spoon-feeding information to students; it's about guiding them on a journey of discovery and self-discovery. Encourage curiosity, foster creativity, and empower students to think critically, solve problems, and explore new ideas.

The best lessons are often learned through laughter, so don't be afraid to inject a little humor into your teaching!

# Drawing Inspiration from the Teaching Community

(Because Everyone has an Opinion)

*"In the classroom, as in life, we must stand up for what is right, even when it is difficult. Our students count on us to be their advocates, champions, and voices."*

**- Holly DiBella-McCarthy**

Teaching is not just a job; it's a calling, a passion, and a lifelong commitment to making a difference in the lives of others. Be your students' champion by drawing inspiration from the teaching community, sharing your experiences, and learning from your fellow educators' collective wisdom and expertise. Remember, you're not alone on this journey. Together, we can overcome any obstacle, tackle any challenge, and transform the world, one student at a time.

# BENEFITS

of "Kid Quotes" Journaling

# Why Kid Quotes Are Better Than Coffee

(Seriously, They're Hilarious)

There's nothing quite like children's hilarious and often profound insights to brighten your day and remind you of why you became a teacher in the first place.

From witty one-liners to unexpected observations, kid quotes are guaranteed to bring a smile to your face and warm your heart.

Start a kid quotes journal to capture these priceless moments and treasure them. Trust me, they're better than coffee for perking up your spirits on those long, challenging days in the classroom!

# How Kid Quotes Can Save Your Sanity

### (And Provide Endless Entertainment)

Let's face it, teaching can be tough, but kid quotes are like a ray of sunshine on even the darkest of days.

When you're feeling overwhelmed, stressed, or just plain exhausted, take a moment to read through your kid quotes journal and remind yourself of the joy, laughter, and wonder that fills your classroom every day.

Not only will it lift your spirits and boost your morale, but it will also provide endless entertainment and inspiration for years to come.

# The Dos and Don'ts of Kid Quotes Journaling

(Spoiler Alert: There Are No Don'ts)

When it comes to kid quotes journaling, there are no rules, guidelines, or limits to your creativity.

Write them down on sticky notes, record them in a notebook, or create a digital scrapbook to share with friends and family. Get creative, have fun, and embrace the joy of capturing these priceless childhood innocence and wisdom moments.

The only rule of kid quotes journaling is never to stop collecting and cherishing these precious memories.

# KID QUOTES

"I want to be a princess and a firefighter!"

"My mommy said she's proud of me because I ate all my vegetables, even the green ones that taste like grass."

"When I get big, I'm going to build a robot that does my chores."

"Why does the baby get to cry all the time and still be the boss?"

"I'm not sleepy, and I'm just practicing my blink-dance."

"I feel a squirrel circus in my tummy!"

"I was mad, and steam almost came out of my ears and I thought my head might actually turn into a volcano and explode!"

"The dog really did eat it! Oh, did you hear that one before?"

As you step into the world of teaching, remember the incredible impact you hold in your hands. Embrace the challenges, celebrate the victories, and never underestimate the power of a kind word or a listening ear. Keep your sense of humor close, your passion burning bright and always believe in the limitless potential of every student who walks through your door. And as you navigate the joys and challenges of teaching, don't forget to capture the priceless moments—the laughter, the insights, and the unexpected gems—with Kid Quotes.

Use the next few pages to document these treasures this school year.

*"I can shake off everything as I write;*
*my sorrows disappear,*
*my courage is reborn."*
**- Anne Frank**

# MY CLASS
# KID QUOTES

KID QUOTE

*quotes & notes*

*To New Beginnings*

KID QUOTE

*quotes & notes*

KID QUOTE

*quotes & notes*

*To New Beginnings*

KID QUOTE

*quotes & notes*

KID QUOTE

*quotes & notes*

*To New Beginnings*

## KID QUOTE
## *quotes & notes*

KID QUOTE

*quotes & notes*

*To New Beginnings*

KID QUOTE

*quotes & notes*

KID QUOTE

## *quotes & notes*

KID QUOTE

*quotes & notes*

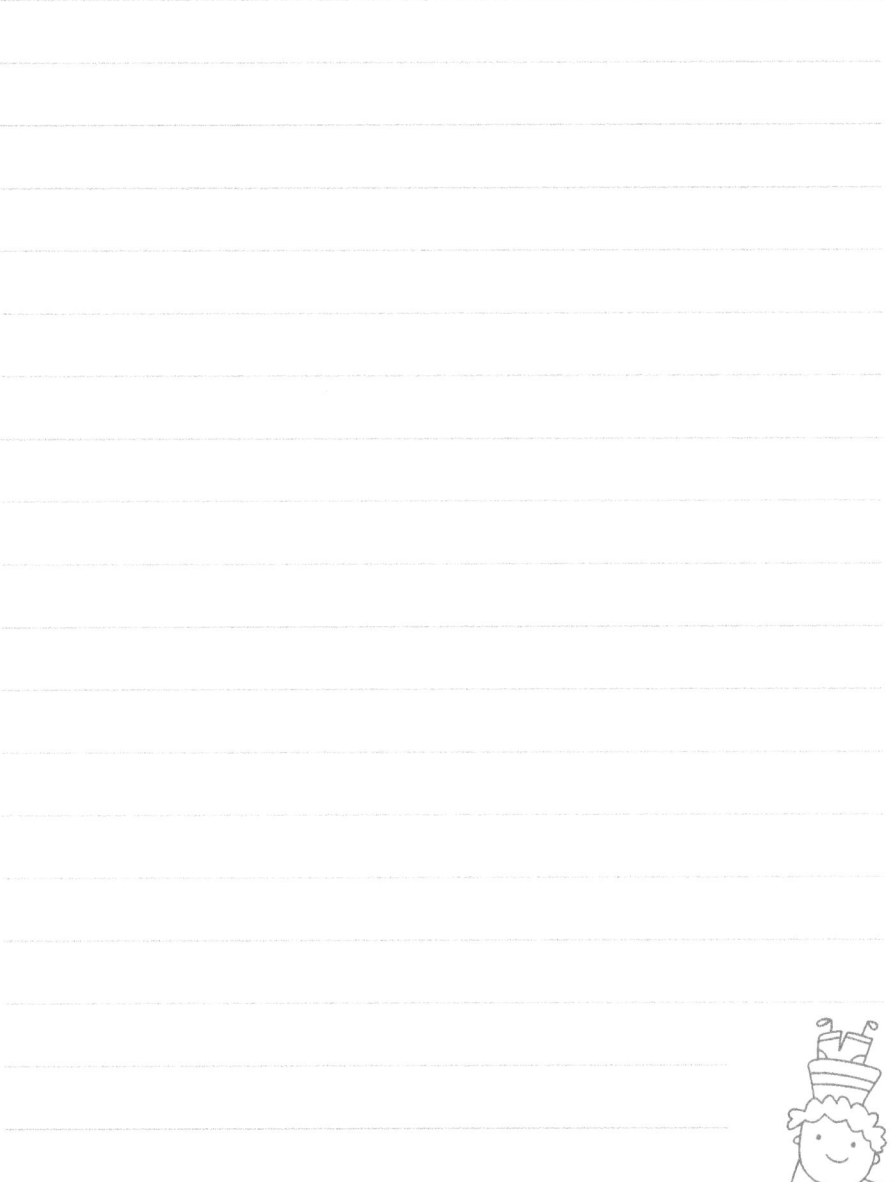

KID QUOTE

*quotes & notes*

*To New Beginnings*

KID QUOTE

*quotes & notes*

# KID QUOTE

## *quotes & notes*

## KID QUOTE

## *quotes & notes*

KID QUOTE

*quotes & notes*

*To New Beginnings*

# KID QUOTE

## *quotes & notes*

# KID QUOTE
## *quotes & notes*

## KID QUOTE

## *quotes & notes*

KID QUOTE

## *quotes & notes*

*To New Beginnings*

KID QUOTE

*quotes & notes*

## KID QUOTE

## *quotes & notes*

*To New Beginnings*

KID QUOTE

*quotes & notes*

# KID QUOTE

## *quotes & notes*

*To New Beginnings*

KID QUOTE

*quotes & notes*

KID QUOTE

*quotes & notes*

*To New Beginnings*

KID QUOTE

*quotes & notes*

KID QUOTE

*quotes & notes*

*To New Beginnings*

## KID QUOTE

## *quotes & notes*

## KID QUOTE

*quotes & notes*

*To New Beginnings*

KID QUOTE

*quotes & notes*

# KID QUOTE

## *quotes & notes*

*To New Beginnings*

KID QUOTE

*quotes & notes*

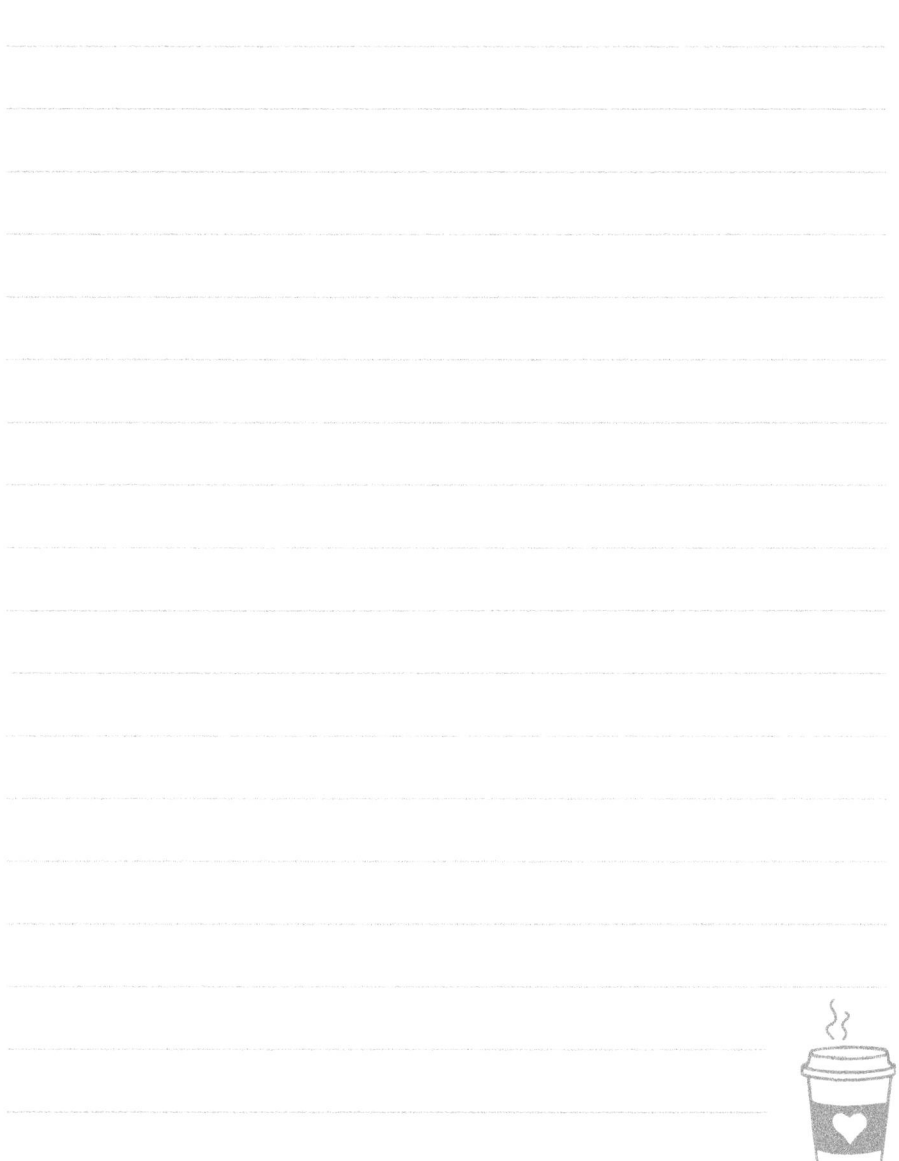

## KID QUOTE

## *quotes & notes*

KID QUOTE

*quotes & notes*

Meet Holly DiBella-McCarthy, a seasoned educator and former public school administrator with a passion for early childhood and special education.

Having taught from pre-K through college, she brings a wealth of experience and insight to her writing. Now a full-time author, Holly channels her expertise into crafting engaging and informative books for both adults and children. From educational resources for educators and parents to heartwarming picture books for young readers, her work reflects her dedication to making a difference in the world of education.

www.hollydibellamccarthy.com

www.bookchatterpress.com

Free Resources and Blog Articles
for parents and teachers

holly@bookchatterpress.com

Your Review Matters

# More Books By
## Holly DiBella-McCarthy

Dilly Duck Plays All Day
Dilly Duck Plans a Parade
Dilly Duck Saves the Day

Picture Books for ages 3-7

Dilly and Pals See Me Read
Level 1 Reader

Parenting with a Teacher's Toolbox:
Practical Strategies for Success

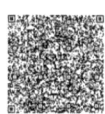

Book Folding for Beginners
More Book Folding for Beginners

# NOTEWORTHY

# TO DO LIST
ONE STEP AT A TIME.
YOU'LL GET THERE

## TO DO LIST
ONE STEP AT A TIME.
YOU'LL GET THERE

www.ingramcontent.com/pod-product-compliance
Lightning Source LLC
Chambersburg PA
CBHW052033030426
42337CB00027B/4985